Learn About

YOUR BEST SELF

I Can Be Brave

written by Meredith Rusu

illustrated by Alexandra Colombo

Children's Press®

An imprint of Scholastic Inc.

Special thanks to Doctor Ann (Nancy) Close, assistant professor at the Yale School of Medicine and member of the Child Study Center at Yale University, for her insight into the development of children in early childhood.

Library of Congress Cataloging-in-Publication Data available
ISBN 978-93-5954-354-3

This reprint edition: September, 2025

Printed in India at Shiv Shakti Printing & Trading Co., Haryana

Book design by Kathleen Petelinsek

TABLE OF CONTENTS

I Can Be Brave

Hi! My name is Luís, and I like being **brave**! It's not always easy. Sometimes it can even be a little scary. But when I work hard to be brave, I feel proud and strong.

BRAVERY IS A *SUPERPOWER*!

Let me show you some ways I can be brave.

Fairy Tales
Once upon a time there
was a small
in the woods
surrounded
by many

I can be brave when I try a new vegetable, like eggplant. It has a funny name and doesn't even look like an egg.

But it turns out that it's super tasty!

BRAVERY IS A SUPERPOWER!

Because of me, my little sister wants to try eggplant, too!

I can be brave by telling the truth, even if I might get in trouble.

When I tell the truth, grown-ups know they can trust me.

All superheroes need to be **trustworthy**!

BRAVERY IS A SUPERPOWER!

Even though my mommy is disappointed, she's proud I told the truth.

I can be brave by getting back on my bike after I fall.

The scrapes sting. But the only way to become a super rider is to keep trying.

BRAVERY IS A SUPERPOWER!

Seeing me get back up gives my friends the courage to get back up when they fall, too.

I can be brave by staying still while the doctor gives me a shot.

Getting shots makes me feel nervous.

But I tell myself the medicine will make me stronger, like a real superhero.

BRAVERY IS A SUPERPOWER!

My friends like my bandage and feel brave when they get shots, too!

I can be brave by telling another kid to stop teasing me about my lunch.

His words hurt. But I use my **confident** superhero voice. That makes me feel strong!

BRAVERY IS A SUPERPOWER!

My friends also stand up for themselves if somebody makes fun of them!

I can be brave by finishing my school report on spiders. Even though they really creep me out, they're also super interesting.

BRAVERY IS A SUPERPOWER!

My friends are impressed by all my cool spider facts and want to learn more!

EVACUATION PLAN
EXIT
EXIT
ALARM BUTTON
WAY TO RUN
FIRE EX.
FIRE ALARM
RING R

I can be brave by following **directions** during a fire drill.

If I stay calm and listen, I'm helping to keep everyone safe.

And that's extra super!

BRAVERY IS A SUPERPOWER!

My friends follow my lead and listen to the teacher.

I can be brave by **performing** onstage in the school play.

I am worried about forgetting my lines. But I've practiced really hard.

And performing feels exciting!

BRAVERY IS A SUPERPOWER!

If we're brave together, the show will be a super success!

I can be brave by having a sleepover at grandma and grandpa's house when my moms travel for work.

I'll miss them while they're away.

But I know they're doing super jobs.

BRAVERY IS A SUPERPOWER!

My little sister will trust everything is all right because of me!

It's not always easy being brave.

But when you are, it's a super feeling!

Will you give it a try?

I'll bet it can be your superpower, too!

WHAT IS BRAVERY?

There are lots of different ways to be brave! Sometimes being brave means doing things that are scary. Other times it means having the courage to do what's right.

With an adult, take a look at the examples that follow. Which sound like "the scary thing"? Which sound like "the right thing"?

1
Competing in a contest for the first time.

2
Staying calm when you see a huge bug on the wall.

3

Being honest when a teacher asks you if you dropped the glass jar on the floor.

4

Wearing an outfit that you like, but others might think is different.

5

Trusting everything will be okay if your family moves to a new town.

6

Admitting you fibbed about something, like saying you washed your hands when you didn't.

7

Going to a birthday party where you do not know anyone.

Now, think about this: How would you be brave in each of these situations?

ANSWERS: Numbers 1, 2, 4, 5, and 7 are "the scary thing." Numbers 3 and 6 are "the right thing."

FIND YOUR SUPERPOWER!

Try these ways of being brave every day!

When you visit someone's house, say hi to everyone, even if you feel shy.

Try one new food each week. If you're super brave, try a new food each day!

Don't give up when something is tricky, like tying your shoes or learning to jump rope. Keep trying!

If a classmate looks especially sad, ask them what's wrong. And listen to what they say. You might be the super friend they need!

Give a new activity a chance. Or ask your parents if you can try something you've never done before, like karate.

Forgive someone when they make a mistake. It takes courage to give someone a second chance.

GLOSSARY

admitting (ad-MIT-ing) telling the truth about something you did or something that happened that was wrong

Sonia felt guilty admitting she had taken the cookie from the cookie jar.

brave (BRAYV) having the courage to face danger, difficulty, or pain

You were brave to tell him to stop picking on Joe.

confident (KAHN-fi-duhnt) self-assured; having a strong belief in your own abilities

Tawanda is a confident swimmer.

courage (KUR-ij) the ability to do something that scares you

It takes a lot of courage to sing onstage in front of people.

directions (duh-REK-shuhnz) guidance or supervision

Pablo followed the directions for the project.

performing (pur-FORM-ing) acting in a way to entertain an audience

Our class will be performing a play during the Spring Festival.

superpower (SOO-pur-pou-ur) an extraordinary ability beyond those of an ordinary human, such as incredible strength or the ability to fly

My favorite heroine has the superpower of speed.

trustworthy (TRUHST-wur-thee) able to be trusted and relied on to do what is right

The librarian knew Cathy was trustworthy enough to bring the book back.

ABOUT THE AUTHOR

Meredith Rusu has written more than 100 children's books. She lives in New Jersey with her husband and two young sons whom she tries (very hard!) to inspire to be brave every day.

ABOUT THE ILLUSTRATOR

Alexandra Colombo has illustrated more than 100 books that have been published all over the world. She loves walking in the woods, writing poetry, and discovering new places. She lives in Italy with her turtle, Carlo, and her dog, Ary.